9/10/13

From: Daddy 🙂

I Love You
My Little Princess

PETEY YIKES!

by Carter Conlon
illustrated by Treg McCoy
and Erika Thomas

It was a hot July day in Manhattan.

Nobody knows why Petey was standing under a parked car or how he got there.

Maybe the street was too hot for his little bird feet.

"…When you were still under the fig tree, I saw you."
— JOHN 1:48 (AMP) —

Two very kind ladies were on their way home.
One was kind of taller
and one was sort of smaller.

Suddenly, one of them saw Petey standing there.

"YIKES!" thought Petey.

He was always nervous
when people looked at him.

"Do you ever get
nervous when people
look at you?"

"But You, O God, the Lord,
deal kindly with me…"

— PSALM 109:21 (NASB) —

A gentle hand reached out to Petey.
"YiKES!" he said.

Yet before he knew it, Petey was standing on
the kindest hand he had ever felt.

Maybe hands had not always been kind to Petey.

How surprised the very kind ladies were
when Petey began to dance!

He always did funny, twitchy things
when something new came along.

PETEY YIKES!

PETEY YIKES!

PETEY YIKES!

One of the very kind ladies was married to a kind man.
They had a special bird house in their apartment.

The kind man was sad
because the bird house was empty.

The elevator door opened.

Petey went "**Yikes!**"
He was in the nicest place he had ever been.

The kind man saw Petey and said,
"Well, well, well, what have we here?"
The kind man picked up Petey.

Petey began to dance.
Everyone smiled with delight.

"Why do you think everyone smiled?"

"...no one is able to snatch them out of the Father's hand."

— JOHN 10:29 (NASB) —

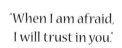

"When I am afraid,
I will trust in you."

— PSALM 56:3 (NIV) —

The kind man had a dog.
The dog's name was Rocky.

It was the scariest dog Petey had ever seen.

"YIKES! YIKES! YIKES!"
shouted Petey.

"Oh no, no, no!" smiled the kind man.
"Rocky only looks scary.
He really is sometimes as afraid as you are."

The kind man began to sing a song... ♪ ♪ ♫

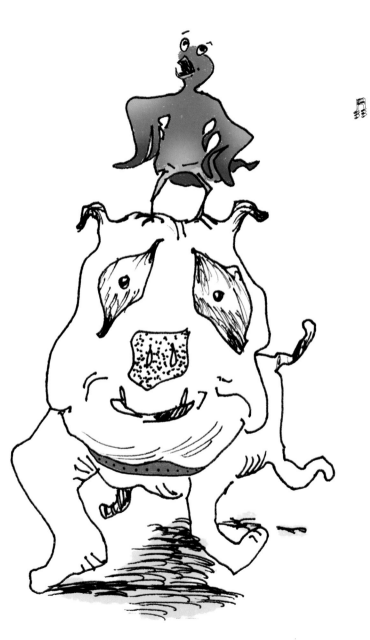

THERE'S A DOGGY,
THERE'S A DOGGY,
THERE'S A DOGGY
IN THE HOUSE!

THERE'S A DOGGY,
THERE'S A DOGGY
IN THE HOUSE!

HE LOOKS LIKE A TIGER,
BUT HE'S CHICKEN
AS A MOUSE!

THERE'S A DOGGY,
THERE'S A DOGGY
IN THE HOUSE!

"For God hath not given us the spirit of fear;
but of power, and of love, and of a sound mind."
— 2 TIMOTHY 1:7 (KJV) —

"In my Father's house
are many mansions:
if it were not so,
I would have told you.
I go to prepare a place for yo[u]

— JOHN 14:2 (KJV) —

The kind man showed Petey his new bird home.
It was the finest house Petey had ever seen.

It was
filled with
branches
and bells
and
wonderful
smells;
mirrors and
beads and
good-tasting seeds!

Petey, Rocky,
the two very kind ladies,
and the kind man
all became good friends.

One day they all went for a drive in the car.

The kind man and the two very kind ladies sang silly songs.
Petey and Rocky laughed and danced until they fell down.

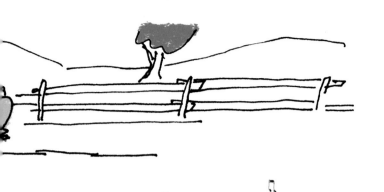

WE COULDN'T FIGURE OUT WHAT HAPPENED.
WE <u>THINKED</u>, WE <u>THANK</u>, WE <u>THUNK</u>.
BUT DADDY PRESSED THE GAS,
THE CAR WENT ...VROOOOM!
AND THE DOGGY IN THE BACK
WENT "**klunk!**"

DADDY PRESSED THE GAS
THE CAR WENT ...VROOOOM!
AND THE DOGGY IN THE BACK
WENT "**klunk!**"

DADDY PRESSED THE GAS,
THE CAR WENT ...VROOOOM!
AND THE DOGGY IN THE BACK
WENT "**klunk!**"

THE DOGGY IN THE BACK WENT "**klunk!**"
THE DOGGY IN THE BACK WENT
"**klunk!**"

CAN YOU FIGURE OUT WHAT HAPPENED?
WE'VE TRIED AND TRIED ALL DAY
WE DROPPED OUR TOYS AND MADE SUCH NOISE
BUT STILL THERE IS NO WAY
THE ONLY SOUND THAT WE HAVE FOUND
IS <u>PLINK</u> AND <u>PLANK</u> AND <u>PLUNK</u>,
BUT...

DID HE HIT HIS TOOTH ON THE WINDOW?
OR KNOCK HIS KNEE ON THE DOOR?
DID HE SPIN 'ROUND AND 'ROUND
AND SLIDE TO THE GROUND
OR SIMPLY FALL ON THE FLOOR?

DADDY PRESSED THE GAS
THE CAR WENT ...VROOOOM!
AND THE DOGGY IN THE BACK
WENT "**klunk!**"

Petey was happy!

Being in the car was so
different than being under it!

He wanted to dance now because he was so happy!

"The Lord is my strength and my song; he has become my salvation."

— PSALM 118:14 (NIV) —

"…the joy of the Lord is your strength."

— NEHEMIAH 8:10 (NIV) —

The End.

Dedicated to Teresa Conlon and Catherine Logan, two very kind ladies.

Copyright © 2006 by Times Square Church
ISBN 0-9789642-0-9

Written by Carter Conlon
Illustration by Treg McCoy
Illustration & Design by Erika Thomas

First printing, 2006
Printed in U.S.A.